THE TEAM BEHIND THE TEAM

Student Athletic-Trainers

NANAKI MATHARU

DEDICATION

I dedicate this book to my mother for always being my rock, my aunt for unconditionally supporting me through every journey, and my dad for providing me with the motivation.

PREFACE

High school sports are one of the most prolific extracurricular activities in America. Athletes put their heart and soul into their sports be it during the practice sessions or during the competitions, trying to win the game or to get starting positions. The physical exercises and athletics always keep the players exposed to the risk of physical injuries that require immediate medical attention and care. This is where the student athletic trainers step in. On-site student athletic trainers in high schools play an enormously important role by responding proactively to prevent, identify and to address the immediate needs resulting from athletic injuries. From being captain for the varsity team of the trainers, to staying in the program, trainers work extremely hard to ensure that athletes receive maximum support and care while playing and performing their best.

Trainers are the group of people that come to the field before the players arrive and are the last ones to leave the ground. During any game or practice session, student athletic trainers are the first people who rush to the field to provide medical aid to the injured athlete. The role and responsibilities of the trainers demands a lot of hard work, dedication, and sacrifice: rain or shine, they are there. It requires lots of mental preparedness and physical strength. Being a student athletic trainer is not an easy job.

As someone who has the experience of being a student athletic trainer in High School, I understand the incredible importance that this role plays and the challenges that come with it. What started as a high school program, student athletic training has become a passion within me that keeps growing with each passing day and, with every step that I take on the field. Through this book, I want to capture and share my innate thoughts and my hands-on experience as a student trainer. I want to provide support and guidance to those who choose to pursue this rewarding and fulfilling program that offers multiple opportunities to make a positive impact on the lives of student -athletes, both on and off the field. This book is not only a guide to the knowledge, skills, and responsibilities of being a successful student athletic trainer, but also a reminder to the importance of taking care of one's physical health while prioritizing mental health along with.

Student athletic trainers exhibit strong and constructive relationships with the players while working closely with coaches, parents, and other healthcare professionals. Through the personalized quality care that they provide, student athletic trainers can meet the individual needs of the athletes and to keep them motivated to perform their best and play fearlessly.

While supporting and imbibing the players with positivity, student athletic trainers continue to keep on gaining knowledge and to keep on honing their own skills in the areas of injury prevention, rehabilitation, nutrition, hydration, physical and mental health. They develop a strong communication and teamwork skills as they work closely with the players and their peers. This book aims to provide a valuable information and practical advice at all levels of being a student athletic trainer.

ACCOLADES

"What does it take to be an athletic trainer, 'to be the first on the field and the last to leave'? Nanaki Matharu, a high school student in Texas, volunteered her time to be a student athletic trainer and learned firsthand what it takes. She then took it one step further and wrote a book summarizing what she learned, sharing her acquired wisdom in the first text of its kind, the perspective of working alongside a certified athletic trainer in a high school as a high school student caring for her peers. More than a concise summary on the job of an athletic trainer, Nanaki Matharu shares her mature beyond her age experience of what it takes to treat the whole student athlete, mind and body, often overlooked by even the best of orthopedic surgeons. For any young student considering a career in athletic training or any field of sports medicine, The Team Behind the Team: Student Athletic-Trainers Book information by Nanaki Matharu is a must read."

-Marc Siberman, MD, NJ Sports Medicine

"I am so very proud of Nanaki and the work she has done in writing this book. I believe it can be a helpful resource for current athletic trainers and can serve as a guide for anyone looking into becoming an athletic trainer. Thank you for sharing your passion with others!"

-Dr. Brad A. Hunt,
Superintendent of Coppell ISD High School

"Extremely informative read! Gives readers a better insight about the roles and responsibilities of student (athletic) trainers and their impact on the team's executive function."

-William Harrington,
Teacher at Coppell High School, Texas

"Nanaki does a great job illustrating the benefits of becoming a Student Athletic Trainer and the importance of their involvement in keeping athletes healthy, both physically and mentally. This book will inspire and equip generations of future athletic trainers and high school sports will benefit from it."

-Zachary Gonzalez, Football Coach
at Coppell High School, Texas

"A true story of how a student used her time positively during the difficult COVID times to do something meaningful for herself, and also to motivate and help others in her class and on the sports field. Nanaki touches upon important aspect of wellbeing on the sports fields, preventative measures and mental health. A must read for all the high school students and especially those engaged in sports and sports medicine."

-Dr. Jaleel Durrani, MD. Chief of Anesthesia,
Director Operating Room, Louisville, KY

TABLE OF CONTENTS

INTRODUCTION

S tudent athletic trainers are the team behind the team. They are the people who get to the field before the playing teams arrive and are the last ones to leave. High school sports play an important part in the lives of students by providing them valuable opportunities for their physical growth and personal growth. However, with the daily practices and competitions at high school sports, comes the risk of injuries that need a proper care and rehabilitation. This is where the student athletic trainers come as a support for the injured players. Student athletic trainers form an integral part of the sports program. They responsibly assess the injury and then effectively and immediately provide care to the athlete.

Student athletic trainers communicate extensively with their coaches and other healthcare professionals to understand the importance of providing effective medical aid and developing training plans for the prevention and rehabilitation that can help reduce the risk of sport injuries while ensuring a safe and timely return to play. The role of student athletic trainers is not only exclusive to the sports injuries, but also to benefit the overall health of the player. Athletic trainers play an important role in educating student-athletes on proper nutrition, hydration, and injury prevention techniques.

To succeed as a student athletic trainer, one must possess a quest for knowledge, empathy and passion. It is important to note that student athletic trainers contribute majorly to the success of high school sports programs and make a big difference in the lives of student athletes. Playing a vital role, student athletic trainers demonstrate critical thinking and analytical reasoning for those who are struggling with mental health issues while fostering a supportive team environment that promotes positive mental health and well-being. Student athletic trainers abide by a set of ethical responsibilities that must be upheld to protect and safeguard the physical as well as mental health of student-athletes. However, the student athletic trainer's role also comes with its own set of challenges that must be navigated to succeed. Time management and prioritization are the key considerations that student athletic trainers must manage while balancing their own academic and extracurricular responsibilities.

CHAPTER 1

THE IMPORTANCE OF INJURY PREVENTION AND REHABILITATION

Injuries are a common occurrence in the world of sports and physical activity and can have a significant impact on an athlete's performance and overall well-being. Therefore, injury prevention and rehabilitation are crucial components of any training program.

Injury Prevention

Injury prevention involves taking proactive measures to reduce the risk of injury during physical activity. A proper warm-up and cool-down routine, appropriate equipment and safety gear, and a proper technique and form are the prerequisites of injury prevention. It is essential to understand that injury prevention is not a one-time event but an ongoing process that requires consistent efforts and attention from the players.

One of the primary benefits of injury prevention is that it helps athletes avoid injuries that can sideline them from their sport or physical activity. Additionally, injury prevention can improve athletes' performance by allowing them to train and compete at their full potential without the fear of injury.

Rehabilitation

Despite the best efforts, injuries can still happen. When they do, rehabilitation becomes essential. Rehabilitation is the process of restoring an athlete's physical health and function after an injury. It involves a combination of medical treatment, physical therapy, and exercise to help the athletes recover fully and return to their sport or activity.

Rehabilitation is crucial because it helps prevent long-term damage and chronic pain resulting from an injury. It also helps athletes regain their confidence and mental strength, which can be just as important as their physical abilities. Moreover, rehabilitation can help athletes identify and address underlying issues that may have contributed to their injury, such as poor technique or muscle imbalances.

The Relationship Between Prevention and Rehabilitation

Injury prevention and rehabilitation are the two sides of the same coin. Without injury prevention, athletes are more likely to experience injuries that require rehabilitation. Without rehabilitation, athletes may not be able to recover fully and return to their sport or activity. Therefore, it is essential to view injury prevention and rehabilitation as complementary processes rather than as separate entities.

Athletes should prioritize injury prevention as a proactive measure to avoid injuries. However, in the event of an injury, rehabilitation should be a priority to ensure a full recovery. Moreover, injury prevention and rehabilitation should be ongoing processes that athletes should incorporate into their training routines to maintain optimal physical health and performance.

CHAPTER 2

MENTAL HEALTH IN HIGH SCHOOL SPORTS

Mental health is an important aspect of the overall well-being for student-athletes. Mental health needs are very crucial to the high school sports programs. Student-athletes not only go through the stress of giving their best performance but also through the gravity arising from how to balance their academic demands and social pressures. Any additional physical injuries can have a significant impact on the mental health of student-athletes and can lead them to feelings of frustration and isolation. This stress can put student-athletes at the risk of mental health issues such as anxiety and depression.

The Role of Athletic Trainers in Supporting Mental Health

Athletic trainers play a crucial role in supporting the mental health of student-athletes. While communicating with the players, trainers instill strong teamwork and encourage open communication within the team. This transparency between the trainers and players results in a healthier and strong bond. As a student athletic trainer, I find these one-to-one open conversations very rewarding and fulfilling. A good communication can have an impact on motivating the player while bringing inner gratification to the student athletic trainer for providing the timely help and support.

Athletic trainers work with student-athletes to develop strategies that cope with stress and anxiety. These strategies may include mindfulness techniques, relaxation exercises, and other stress-reducing practices. Athletic trainers educated on the importance of self-care and stress management that can help student-athletes develop healthy habits that supports their mental well-being.

The Importance of Seeking Professional Help

While athletic trainers can provide valuable support to student-athletes struggling with mental health issues, it is also important to recognize the limitations of their expertise. Athletic trainers are not licensed mental health professionals. They may not have the training or expertise necessary to provide comprehensive mental health care. For a student-athlete struggling with mental health issues, it is important to seek professional help from a licensed mental health professional.

Strategies for Promoting Mental Health and Well-Being on Sports Teams

As a student athletic trainer, you play a vital role in supporting the overall well-being of the sportspersons. Understanding the importance of mental health and having effective strategies in place, can greatly enhance the team's performance, unity, and individual growth. Following these strategies can help you and the team around you.

Educating on Mental Health:

Start by educating yourself and the team about mental health. Discussing common mental health challenges that the athletes may face, such as performance anxiety, stress, and burnout. Providing information on the signs and symptoms of mental health issues by creating an environment where individuals feel comfortable to speak out and to seek help by sharing their experiences.

Fostering a Supportive Environment:

Creating a team culture that values mental health and well-being. Encouraging open communication and empathy among team members. Promoting a supportive and non-judgmental atmosphere where athletes feel safe discussing their struggles without fear of stigmatization. Emphasizing the importance of teamwork and to support one another, both on and off the field.

Incorporating Mindfulness and Relaxation Techniques:

Teaching athletes' mindfulness and relaxation techniques to help manage stress and improve focus. Introducing breathing exercises, meditation, and visualization exercises that can be practiced individually or as a team. Encouraging regular breaks during training sessions or competitions to allow athletes to reset and refocus their minds.

Establishing Clear Communication Channels:

Setting up effective communication channels within the team structure. Encouraging athletes to express their concerns, thoughts, and feelings to you as the athletic trainer or to designated team leaders. Regular check-ins and one-on-one conversations can help identify potential issues early on and offer necessary support. Fostering a culture of trust and confidentiality and ensuring that athletes feel comfortable discussing their mental health.

Encouraging Work-Life Balance:

Helping athletes strike a healthy balance between their sporting commitments and other aspects of their lives. Promoting the importance of self-care, adequate sleep, nutrition, and leisure activities outside of sports. Encourage athletes to pursue hobbies or interests that provide a sense of fulfillment and contribute to their overall well-being. Along with that promoting self-reflection among athletes, encouraging them to understand their own strengths, limitations, and areas for growth. Help them set realistic goals and develop action plans to achieve them. Regularly revisit and assess these goals, adapting them as necessary, to foster a sense of progress and achievement.

Provide Resources and Support:

Equipping yourself with resources to address mental health concerns effectively. Collaborate with mental health professionals, school counselors, or support services to provide referrals and access to appropriate help when needed. Educate athletes on available resources, such as hotlines, counseling services, or workshops, and destigmatize seeking professional help.

Prioritizing mental health and well-being within sports teams is crucial for the overall success and happiness of athletes. By implementing these strategies, you can create a supportive environment that fosters mental resilience, teamwork, and personal growth. Remember, the journey to optimal performance involves not only physical fitness but also nurturing the mind and spirit of each team member.

CHAPTER 3

NUTRITION AND HYDRATION FOR STUDENT-ATHLETES

Proper nutrition and hydration are essential for optimal athletic performance. Student-athletes who fuel their bodies with the right nutrients and fluids are better able to perform and recover more quickly from workouts and competitions.

The Importance of Proper Nutrition

Nutrition plays a critical role in athletic performance. Student-athletes who consume a balanced diet that includes a variety of nutrient-dense foods, are better able to meet the energy demands of their sport. Healthy eating habits support muscle growth and faster repair in case of injury. A balanced diet should include:

- **Carbohydrates**: They are the primary fuel source. Student-athletes should consume complex carbohydrates like whole grains, fruits, and vegetables to provide sustained energy throughout their workouts or competitions.

- **Protein:** Protein is essential for muscle growth and repair. Student-athletes should consume lean sources of protein like chicken, fish, beans, and tofu to support muscle recovery and growth.

- **Fat:** Fat is an important energy source for endurance exercises. Student-athletes should consume healthy fats like avocados, nuts, and olive oil to provide sustained energy during long workouts or competitions.

Student-athletes should consume plenty of fruits and vegetables that provide essential vitamins and minerals to the body. It is recommended to avoid processed foods and sugary drinks that can aggravate inflammation and cause energy crashes.

The Importance of Proper Hydration

Proper hydration is essential for the optimal athletic performance. Student-athletes who are dehydrated may experience fatigue, dizziness, and decreased performance. When it comes to participating in sports, especially in hot and humid conditions, understanding heat illness and its relationship to proper hydration and diet is crucial. As a student athletic trainer, your role in educating athletes about the importance of staying hydrated and maintaining a balanced diet cannot be overstated.

Understanding Heat Illness:

Heat illness encompasses a wide range of conditions from mild to severe that occur due to the body's inability to adequately dissipate heat. The following are the different types of heat illnesses:

a. **Heat Cramps:**

Heat cramps are painful muscle contractions that occur during or after intense exercise in hot conditions. They are often caused by electrolyte imbalances and dehydration. Athletes experiencing heat cramps should rest in a cool area, rehydrate with fluids containing electrolytes, and gently stretch and massage the affected muscles.

b. **Heat Exhaustion:**

Heat exhaustion is a more severe form of heat illness and is characterized by symptoms such as excessive sweating, weakness, dizziness, headache, nausea, and rapid heartbeat. It can occur due to the prolonged exposure to heat and inadequate fluids and electrolytes replacement. Immediate measures for someone with heat exhaustion include moving to a cool place, loosening clothing, applying cool compresses, rehydrating with fluids, and seeking medical attention if symptoms worsen.

c. **Heat Syncope:**

Heat syncope, also known as heat collapse, is a temporary loss of consciousness or fainting that typically happens during or after physical exertion in high temperatures. It occurs due to a sudden drop in blood pressure caused by dehydration and inadequate blood flow to the brain. Treatment involves moving the individual to a cool, shaded area, elevating the legs, and providing fluids.

d. Heat Stroke:

Heat stroke is the most severe and life-threatening form of heat illness. It occurs when the body's core temperature rises above 104°F (40°C) and the body's heat-regulating mechanisms fail. Symptoms include high body temperature, altered mental state, confusion, rapid breathing, rapid heart rate, and potentially seizures or loss of consciousness. Heat stroke is a medical emergency requiring immediate professional medical attention. While awaiting medical help, move the person to a cooler place, remove excess clothing, and cool the body using methods such as cold-water immersion or applying ice packs.

Hydration as a Key Preventative Measure:

Proper hydration is one of the most effective ways to prevent heat illness. Athletes should maintain a consistent fluid intake before, during, and after physical activity, especially in hot environments. Encourage athletes to drink water frequently, even if they don't feel thirsty, as thirst is not always a reliable indicator of hydration status. Emphasize the importance of starting activities already well-hydrated and continuing to hydrate throughout training or competition.

The Role of Electrolytes:

In addition to water, electrolytes play a significant role in maintaining proper hydration. Electrolytes, such as sodium, potassium, and magnesium, help regulate fluid balance and muscle function. Encourage athletes to consume sports drinks or electrolyte-rich fluids during prolonged activities or intense training sessions to replenish both fluids and electrolytes lost through sweat.

Heat illness is a serious concern for athletes, but with the right knowledge and practice, it can be mitigated. By understanding the different types of heat illnesses and their symptoms, educating athletes about hydration and nutrition, and by implementing practical strategies, student athletic trainer can contribute to a safer and more successful athletic experience for all. Prioritizing proper hydration and a balanced diet will not only help prevent heat-related issues but also help in optimized performance and overall well-being of the players.

Developing Healthy habits:

- Trainers and athletes should plan their meals and snacks ahead of time to ensure that they are properly energized.

- Eat a variety of foods that are good for maintaining the energy levels while playing.

- Drinking water and intaking fluids throughout the day. Student-athletes should aim to drink at least eight glasses of water each day to stay hydrated. Take plenty of water before, during, and after exercise maintains hydration levels and replenishes the lost minerals and salts.

- Monitoring of the urine color: Urine color can be a good indicator of hydration levels. Student-athletes should aim for a pale-yellow color.

- Seek guidance from a healthcare professional: Student-athletes who are unsure about their nutrition or hydration needs should seek guidance from a healthcare professional, such as an athletic trainer or dietitian.

Understanding Eating Disorders in Athletes

While sports promote physical health and well-being, they can also put athletes at risk of developing unhealthy relationships with food and body image.

1. **The Prevalence and Risk Factors:**

   Eating disorders, such as anorexia nervosa, bulimia nervosa, and binge eating disorder, affect athletes across various sports and genders. Understand the risk factors that make athletes susceptible to these disorders, including performance pressure, body image concerns, perfectionism, and the pursuit of a specific body shape or weight for optimal athletic performance. Recognize that the prevalence of eating disorders is not confined to a specific sport or level of competition, and vigilance is essential across all athletic disciplines.

2. **Impact on Physical and Mental Health:**

    Eating disorders can have severe consequences on both physical and mental health. Athletes may experience fatigue, weakness, and an increased risk of injuries due to inadequate nutrient intake. Moreover, mental health can be profoundly affected, leading to anxiety, depression, social isolation, and a decline in athletic performance. Try to educate athletes, coaches, and the sports medicine team about the potential consequences of eating disorders, emphasizing that proper nutrition is vital for overall athletic success and well-being.

3. **Early Identification and Intervention:**

    Even though it may not be your responsibility to identify eating disorders, creating a safe space and open end of communication is imperative. Early identification of eating disorders is crucial for preventing further harm and initiating appropriate interventions. Encourage the implementation of routine screenings for disordered eating behaviors and body image concerns among athletes. Create an open and non-judgmental environment where athletes feel comfortable discussing their struggles with food and body image. Ensure that coaches and sports medicine professionals receive training in recognizing warning signs and referring athletes to specialized eating disorder professionals for evaluation and treatment.

4. **Promoting a Balanced Approach to Nutrition:**

Empower athletes with accurate information about nutrition and the importance of fueling their bodies appropriately for athletic performance and recovery. Promote a balanced approach to nutrition, emphasizing the role of various food groups and the importance of listening to hunger and fullness cues. Discourage restrictive diets, fad eating patterns, and extreme weight loss methods. Instead, foster a culture of support, where athletes feel encouraged to make healthy choices that nourish their bodies and enhance their athletic abilities.

5. **Providing Resources and Education:**

Make resources and educational materials on eating disorders readily available to athletes, coaches, and parents. Organize workshops, seminars, and presentations on topics related to nutrition, body image, and mental health in sports. Raise awareness about the prevalence of eating disorders and emphasize the significance of early intervention and treatment.

Addressing eating disorders in athletes requires a multidisciplinary approach that includes education, early identification, intervention, and the creation of a supportive team environment. As part of the sports medicine community, we have a responsibility to prioritize the well-being of athletes by promoting a balanced approach to nutrition and fostering a positive body image. By equipping athletes with the knowledge and support they need, we can empower them to thrive not only as athletes but also as healthy, confident individuals.

Recognizing the Difference from Eating Disorders

While disordered eating shares similarities with eating disorders, it is essential to understand the distinction between the two. It is crucial to know the characteristics of disordered eating, its potential impact on athletes' physical and mental health, and the significance of early intervention. By recognizing the difference between disordered eating and eating disorders, we can better support athletes and foster a culture of balanced nutrition and well-being in the sports community.

1. **Disordered Eating Defined:**

    Disordered eating refers to a range of irregular eating behaviors that do not meet the diagnostic criteria for a specific eating disorder but can still negatively impact an individual's overall health and well-being. These behaviors may include restrictive dieting, skipping meals, excessive calorie counting, frequent weight fluctuations, and feelings of guilt or shame related to food choices. Disordered eating patterns often emerge from factors such as body image concerns, pressure to achieve a specific weight or body shape, or a desire to optimize athletic performance.

2. **Recognizing the Difference from Eating Disorders:**

While disordered eating shares similarities with eating disorders, the primary distinction lies in the severity and persistence of behaviors. Eating disorders, such as anorexia nervosa, bulimia nervosa, and binge eating disorder, involve more pervasive and severe patterns of disordered eating, accompanied by profound physical and mental health consequences. Eating disorders often require specialized treatment and support from healthcare professionals, whereas disordered eating may respond to early interventions and changes in behaviors.

Understanding the difference between disordered eating and eating disorders is vital for identifying and addressing potential issues among athletes. By recognizing disordered eating behaviors early on and providing timely support, we can prevent the escalation of harmful patterns and promote a positive and balanced approach to nutrition and well-being. As part of the sports medicine community, we play a crucial role in fostering an environment that prioritizes the overall health and success of athletes, both on and off the field.

CHAPTER 4

THE ETHICAL RESPONSIBILITIES OF STUDENT ATHLETIC TRAINERS

A Student Athletic trainers role comes a set of ethical responsibilities that must be upheld to protect the health and safety of student-athletes. Being a trainer requires a strong and disciplined approach to set ground rules for oneself and for the athletes. Student athletic trainers should adhere to the obligations to protect the health and safety of student-athletes by following and displaying professional standards of practice, maintaining confidentiality, and recognizing the limits of their expertise.

Protecting the Health and Safety of Student-Athletes

The primary ethical responsibility of student athletic trainers is to protect the health and safety of student-athletes. The trainers should always have a strong preparedness plan with them to handle emergency situations arising during the physical activity. There should be a willingness to develop a sense of ethical responsibility by constantly educating oneself and staying up to date on the latest research and best practices in injury prevention and rehabilitation. They must be knowledgeable about the human body, anatomy, and physiology, as well as injury prevention and rehabilitation techniques. Additionally, they must be able to recognize the signs and symptoms of injuries and know how to respond appropriately.

Adhering to Professional Standards of Practice

Athletic trainers are held to professional standards of practice that govern their behavior and actions in the workplace. These standards are designed to ensure that athletic trainers provide quality care to their players and uphold the integrity of the program. Student athletic trainers must adhere to these standards to maintain their certifications such as BLS (Basic Life Support) and Heart saver.

The National Athletic Trainers' Association (NATA) has established a code of ethics for athletic trainers that outlines the ethical responsibilities. The code of ethics includes principles such as:

- The athletic trainer shall respect the rights, welfare, and dignity of all individuals.
- The athletic trainer shall practice within their scope of knowledge and expertise.
- The athletic trainer shall maintain confidentiality and protect the privacy of patients.
- The athletic trainer shall recognize the need for continuing education and professional development.

By adhering to these professional standards of practice, student athletic trainers can ensure that they are providing quality care to student-athletes and upholding the integrity of the program.

Maintaining Confidentiality

Athletic trainers are responsible for maintaining the confidentiality of their players. This includes protecting the privacy of player records, medical information, and personal information. Student athletic trainers must maintain confidentiality in accordance with federal and state laws, as well as professional standards of practice.

Confidentiality is important for several reasons. First, it protects the privacy of players and helps to build trust between the players and the healthcare provider. Second, it ensures that sensitive medical information is not shared with unauthorized individuals. Finally, it is required by law in accordance with HIPAA.

Recognizing the Limits of Their Expertise

It is very important for a student athletic trainer to understand and recognize the limits their knowledge and expertise. Athletic trainers are not medical doctors. Similarly, student trainers may not have the training or expertise necessary to diagnose and treat all types of injuries and illnesses. Referring players to healthcare professionals is not only an ethical responsibility of athletic trainers, but it is also a legal requirement in many cases. Athletic trainers must ensure that all medical decisions are made in the best interest of the athlete.

CHAPTER 5

THE SKILLS NECESSARY TO SUCCEED AS A STUDENT ATHLETIC TRAINER

The success of a student athletic trainer lies primarily on a combination of knowledge, skills, and passion. While it is a very fulfilling and inspiring role, at the same time it can get very stressful while dealing with emergency situations. The athletic trainers have to stay calm knowing there is an urgency, have to be compassionate yet assertive and most important they have to be friends yet disciplined.

The Drive to Knowledge

As a student athletic trainer, your journey in sports medicine involves more than just practical skills—it is an opportunity to develop a thirst for knowledge and continuous learning.

Embracing Intellectual Curiosity:

Intellectual curiosity serves as the foundation for the drive to knowledge. It is the inherent desire to explore, question, and seek deeper understanding. As a high school athletic trainer, embrace this curiosity by actively engaging with the field of sports medicine. Emphasize the importance of asking questions, seeking answers, and challenging assumptions. Encourage a mindset that fosters new ideas, perspectives, and research, allowing curiosity to fuel your quest for knowledge.

Cultivating Lifelong Learning:

Recognize that the drive to knowledge is a lifelong journey. While your high school years provide a solid foundation, they are just the beginning. Commit to a mindset of continuous learning and growth. Stay updated with the latest research, advancements, and best practices in sports medicine. Seek out opportunities for professional development, attend workshops, conferences, and seminars, and engage with mentors and experts who can broaden your understanding. During your time in the program, you will have to complete the tasks and assignments necessary to earn your various certifications.

Exploring Diverse Disciplines:

Expand your knowledge base by exploring various disciplines related to sports medicine. While your primary focus is athletic training, it is beneficial to have a well-rounded understanding of other relevant fields. Learn about anatomy, physiology, biomechanics, nutrition, psychology, and other disciplines that intersect with sports medicine. Understanding the connection between these fields will enhance the ability to provide comprehensive care and better serve high school athletes.

Engaging with Technology and Research:

Embrace the advancements in technology and research within sports medicine. Stay informed about emerging technologies, diagnostic tools, and treatment modalities that can revolutionize the field. Engage with research studies, case studies, and academic journals to deepen your understanding and contribute to the collective knowledge of high school athletic training. Incorporate evidence-based practices into your work and adapt your approach based on new information and insights.

Collaboration and Networking:

Recognize the power of collaboration and networking in the pursuit of knowledge. Engage with professionals, fellow athletic trainers, coaches, and healthcare providers to exchange ideas, share experiences, and learn from one another. Attend conferences, workshops, and industry events to connect with individuals who can expand your perspectives and challenge your thinking. Collaborative efforts foster an environment of growth and contribute to the collective knowledge of the high school athletic training community.

Applying Knowledge in Practice:

Remember that knowledge is most valuable when applied in practical settings. As a high school athletic trainer, seek opportunities to apply what you've learned in real-world scenarios. Work closely with athletes, observe injuries, assess conditions, and develop treatment plans. Reflect on your experiences, analyze outcomes, and adapt your approach based on new information and insights gained. This application of knowledge will enhance your skills and elevate your effectiveness as an athletic trainer.

Be an inspiration:

The drive to knowledge is not only about personal growth but also about inspiring others to embark on their own journeys. Share your knowledge and experiences with fellow student athletic trainers, aspiring professionals, and high school athletes. Mentor and guide them in their pursuit of knowledge, encouraging them to embrace curiosity, continuous learning, and the transformative power of knowledge. By inspiring others, you contribute to the growth and development of the next generation of high school athletic trainers.

Nurturing intellectual curiosity is vital for high school athletic trainers. By embracing curiosity, cultivating lifelong learning, exploring diverse disciplines, engaging with technology and research, fostering collaboration, applying knowledge in practice, and inspiring others, you will foster personal growth and make a meaningful impact in the field of high school sports medicine. The drive to knowledge will not only shape your own path but also contribute to the advancement and elevation of the athletic training profession in the high school setting.

Communication and Teamwork Skills

Strong communication and teamwork skills are the building elements to the foundation of student athletic training. Athletic trainers must be able to communicate effectively with a wide range of individuals, including student-athletes, coaches, and parents. They must be able to work effectively as part of a team, collaborating with others to develop and implement injury prevention and rehabilitation plans.

This can be done through coursework in communication and teamwork. It is important to gain practical experience working in a healthcare setting. This can be done through internships, volunteer work, or shadowing that provide opportunities to work with people and better develop an understanding of their needs and challenges. Athletic trainers must be able to adapt their communication style to meet the needs of different individuals, such as student-athletes who may be experiencing anxiety or stress related to their injury.

Passion for Helping Others

As a trainer, you extend beyond physical care and rehabilitation. It involves providing emotional support, building relationships, and being a pillar of strength for high school athletes facing physical and emotional challenges.

- **The Innate Desire to Help Others:**

  Having a genuine desire to help others is a fundamental quality that lays the groundwork for a successful beginning in sports medicine. Reflect on the reasons that initially sparked your interest in becoming an athletic trainer. Perhaps it was witnessing the positive impact of sports medicine on someone's life or the joy of making a difference in the lives of others. Embrace and nurture this innate desire as it will serve as the driving force behind your passion for helping others.

- **Developing Empathy:**

Empathy, the ability to understand and share the feelings of others, is a critical component of helping others effectively. Cultivate empathy by placing yourself in the shoes of high school athletes and recognizing the challenges they face physically, emotionally, and mentally. Seek to understand their unique circumstances, struggles, and aspirations. By developing empathy, you can better connect with athletes and provide personalized support that addresses their specific needs.

- **Active Listening:**

Listening attentively is a powerful tool in helping others. Practice active listening by being fully present and engaged in conversations with high school athletes. Give them your undivided attention, listen without judgment, and strive to understand their concerns, fears, and goals. Through active listening, you not only gain valuable insight into their experiences but also validate their feelings and foster a sense of trust and support.

- **Cultivating a Service Mindset:**

Shift your mindset from viewing your role as a job to embracing it as a service to others. Recognize that being an athletic trainer is a privilege and an opportunity to make a positive impact on the lives of high school athletes. Embrace the responsibility to provide exceptional care, guidance, and support. Approach each interaction with a service-oriented mindset, seeking ways to meet athletes' needs and enhance their overall well-being.

- **Commitment to Continuous Learning:**

To effectively help others, it is vital to stay updated with the latest advancements and best practices in sports medicine. Commit yourself to continuous learning and professional development. Stay informed about current research, emerging therapies, and innovative approaches to injury prevention and rehabilitation. By expanding your knowledge and skills, you can better serve high school athletes and provide them with the most effective and evidence-based care.

- **Embracing Collaboration:**

Recognize that helping others is a collaborative effort. Embrace collaboration with coaches, healthcare professionals, and other members of the sports medicine team. Together, you can provide comprehensive care, share insights, and leverage diverse expertise to support high school athletes in their athletic pursuits. Collaboration fosters a multidisciplinary approach and strengthens the impact of your collective efforts to help others.

- **Making a Lasting Impact:**

  Ultimately, the desire to help others should be driven by the aim to make a lasting impact in the lives of high school athletes. By embodying compassion, empathy, active listening, a service mindset, a commitment to learning, and a spirit of collaboration, you can create a ripple effect of positive change. Your passion for helping others will not only influence the immediate well-being of athletes but will also inspire them to embody compassion and serve as a catalyst for positive change in their communities.

By developing empathy, actively listening, embracing a service mindset, committing to continuous learning, embracing collaboration, and aiming to make a lasting impact, you can channel your passion into transformative actions that can make a lot of difference to your life as well as that of athletes. Let your genuine desire to help others propel you forward as you navigate the challenges and joys of being a high school athletic trainer. Your dedication to helping others will not only enrich the lives of high school athletes but also bring immense fulfillment and purpose to your own journey.

CHAPTER 6

KINESIOLOGY

K inesiology, also known as human kinetics, is the scientific study of human movement. It encompasses the anatomical, physiological, and biomechanical aspects of how the human body moves and functions. As a student athletic trainer, developing a solid understanding of kinesiology is essential for comprehending human movement, identifying potential injuries, and implementing effective rehabilitation strategies.

It is crucial to grasp the fundamental concepts of kinesiology to better comprehend athletic performance, injury prevention, and rehabilitation.

Understanding kinesiology

Understanding human anatomy is a cornerstone of kinesiology. Familiarize yourself with the major skeletal structures, joints, muscles, and their functions. Gain knowledge of muscle origins, insertions, and actions to comprehend how muscles work in coordination to produce movement. Explore the skeletal system and its role in providing stability, support, and leverage during physical activity.

Physiological Considerations:

Delve into the physiological aspects of kinesiology to understand how the body responds and adapts to exercise and physical stress. Explore the cardiovascular system, respiratory system, and energy systems involved in different intensities and durations of exercise. Gain insight into how physiological factors, such as heart rate, oxygen consumption, and energy metabolism, influence athletic performance and recovery.

Biomechanical Principles:

Biomechanics plays a pivotal role in kinesiology, as it examines the mechanical aspects of human movement. Learn the fundamental principles of biomechanics, such as force, motion, and leverage, and their applications in analyzing sports techniques and preventing injuries. Understand concepts like center of gravity, joint mechanics, and movement efficiency to assess and optimize athletic performance.

Movement Analysis:

Develop skills in movement analysis to identify potential biomechanical deficiencies or imbalances in athletes. Learn how to observe and assess movement patterns, analyze gait, and detect faulty mechanics. This knowledge will enable you to provide targeted interventions, corrective exercises, and injury prevention strategies tailored to the specific needs of high school athletes.

Applied Kinesiology in Rehabilitation:

Discover how kinesiology plays a vital role in the rehabilitation process. Explore the principles of therapeutic exercise and functional movement, which involve restoring mobility, strength, and stability following injuries. Learn how to design and implement rehabilitation programs that focus on improving range of motion, muscle strength, proprioception, and neuromuscular control.

Enhancing Athletic Performance:

Harness the power of kinesiology to optimize athletic performance. Explore how knowledge of biomechanics, muscle physiology, and movement analysis can be utilized to refine sports techniques, enhance power, and speed, and reduce the risk of overuse injuries. Understand the importance of proper conditioning, injury prevention strategies, and individualized training programs for high school athletes.

Performance Analysis:

Use kinesiology principles to analyze and evaluate athletic performance. Assess factors such as coordination, power production, efficiency, and body mechanics to identify areas of improvement. Apply knowledge of kinesiology to enhance skill acquisition, optimize movement patterns, and develop effective training plans tailored to the unique needs of high school athletes.

Sports-Specific Considerations:

Recognize that different sports involve distinct movement patterns and demands. Explore how kinesiology can be applied to understand the specific biomechanics and physiological requirements of different sports. Consider factors such as agility, flexibility, strength, and endurance when designing training programs and injury prevention strategies for high school athletes participating in various sports.

Kinesiology serves as the foundation for understanding human movement and its applications in the program. By comprehending the anatomical, physiological, and biomechanical aspects of kinesiology, you will develop a holistic understanding of athletic performance, injury prevention, and rehabilitation. Embrace the principles of kinesiology to analyze movement, optimize performance, and ensure the well-being of high school athletes under your care. With a solid grasp of kinesiology, you can contribute to the success and safety of high school athletes as they strive for excellence in their chosen sports.

CHAPTER 7

THE BENEFITS OF BEING A STUDENT ATHLETIC TRAINER

Gaining Experience

Experience serves as a powerful teacher, allowing you to refine your skills, deepen your knowledge, and to help develop a comprehensive understanding of the field. Being a student athletic trainer is a rewarding and gratifying experience. The benefits of being a student athletic trainer not only includes the opportunity to gain valuable experience but to develop important skills that can help make a positive impact on the lives of others.

Clinical Placements and Internships:

Clinical placements and internships provide invaluable opportunities to gain hands-on experience under the guidance of experienced professionals. Seek out placements in sports clinics, hospitals, or rehabilitation centers that offer exposure to a wide range of athletic injuries and conditions. Engage actively in observing and assisting with assessments, treatment protocols, and rehabilitation programs.

Embrace the opportunity to learn from seasoned practitioners, ask questions, and expand your practical knowledge.

Shadowing experiences provide a unique window into the world of past the sports medicine program. By shadowing experienced athletic trainers, you can observe their expertise in action, gain insights into their decision-making processes, and witness the dynamic interactions with athletes. Shadowing allows you to see firsthand how athletic trainers handle various scenarios, adapt to challenges, and provide personalized care. It is an opportunity to ask questions, learn from their experiences, and immerse yourself in the daily responsibilities of an athletic trainer. Through shadowing, you can acquire valuable knowledge, refine your observational skills, and further solidify your passion for helping others in the field of medicine.

On-Field Experience:

On-field experience is a cornerstone of sports medicine and kinesiology. Actively participate in athletic events, practices, and competitions to gain practical insights into the unique demands and challenges faced by high school athletes. Assist with injury prevention strategies, taping and bracing, and on-site injury evaluations. Be present on the sidelines to provide immediate care and support during games. Embrace the fast-paced nature of on-field experience, where quick decision-making, effective communication, and problem-solving skills are honed.

Collaboration with Coaches and Healthcare Professionals:

Collaboration with coaches and other healthcare professionals nurtures a comprehensive approach to athlete care. Seek opportunities to work alongside coaches, athletic directors, and strength and conditioning specialists to understand the training methodologies, conditioning programs, and performance enhancement strategies employed in high school sports. Collaborate with sports medicine physicians, physical therapists, and nutritionists to gain insights into their specialized areas and develop a well-rounded approach to athlete care.

Workshops, Seminars, and Conferences:

Participating in workshops, seminars, and conferences is an excellent way to expand your knowledge base and stay updated with the latest advancements in sports medicine. Attend sessions conducted by experts in the field, where you can learn about emerging therapies, evidence-based practices, and innovative techniques. Engage in discussions, network with professionals, and seek mentorship opportunities to enhance your understanding and gain new perspectives.

Research and Scholarly Activities:

Engaging in research and scholarly activities allows you to contribute to the body of knowledge in sports medicine while honing your analytical and critical thinking skills. Collaborate with faculty, researchers, or fellow students to undertake research projects related to sports injuries, performance optimization, or rehabilitation strategies. Conduct literature reviews, collect, and analyze data, and present your findings at conferences or publish them in scientific journals. By actively participating in research, you develop a deeper understanding of evidence-based practice and contribute to advancing the field.

Volunteering and Community Outreach:

Volunteering and engaging in community outreach programs provide unique opportunities to serve and support athletes beyond the confines of your immediate sports setting. Offer your expertise and assistance at community events, youth sports programs, or health fairs. Provide educational sessions on injury prevention, proper nutrition, and overall well-being to athletes and their families. By giving back to the community, you develop a broader perspective on the impact of sports medicine and foster meaningful connections with diverse populations.

Reflecting and Applying Lessons Learned:

Reflection is an essential aspect of gaining valuable experience. Take time to reflect on your experiences, identifying the lessons learned, challenges faced, and areas for improvement. Regularly review your experiences to identify patterns, refine your skills, and apply the knowledge gained in future scenarios. Actively seek feedback from mentors, supervisors, and peers to your self-awareness and maximize the benefits of your experiences.

Gaining valuable experience is a transformative process in the program. Embrace the lessons learned, reflect on your experiences, and continuously seek opportunities to grow and evolve as an athletic trainer. With each experience, you become better equipped to provide exceptional care, support, and guidance to high school athletes on their journey to success and well-being.

Skills Development

Problem-Solving and Critical Thinking:

Sport medicine often requires quick thinking and the ability to solve problems on the spot. Cultivate your problem-solving and critical thinking skills to address complex situations effectively. Practice evaluating multiple variables, considering different perspectives, and making informed decisions under pressure. Embrace a proactive mindset, seeking innovative solutions to challenges faced by athletes and the sports medicine team.

Time Management and Organization:

Managing time efficiently and staying organized is essential in the fast-paced environment of the program. Develop strategies for prioritizing tasks, setting realistic goals, and effectively utilizing resources. Embrace technology tools and systems to streamline administrative tasks, maintain accurate records, and ensure timely communication. By honing your time management and organizational skills, you can optimize your productivity and ensure the smooth operation of daily responsibilities.

Flexibility and Adaptability:

Flexibility and adaptability are vital attributes in this program, where situations can change rapidly. Embrace a mindset that embraces change and adapts to unexpected circumstances. Be prepared to adjust treatment plans, modify rehabilitation protocols, and respond swiftly to emergencies. Develop resilience and the ability to navigate ambiguity while maintaining composure and providing steadfast support to athletes.

Interpersonal and Teamwork Skills:

Collaboration and effective teamwork are essential on and off the field. Cultivate strong interpersonal skills, including active listening, empathy, and conflict resolution. Collaborate seamlessly with coaches, healthcare professionals, and athletes' families to ensure comprehensive care. Embrace diversity, respect differing perspectives, and contribute positively to the team dynamic. By fostering a collaborative environment, you enhance the overall well-being and success of the athletes you serve.

Making a Positive Impact on the Lives of Others

Perhaps the most rewarding aspect of this role is the opportunity to support and uplift high school athletes, coaches, and the broader sports community.

Supporting Athletes' Physical and Emotional Well-being:

As a student athletic trainer, you play a vital role in supporting the physical and emotional well-being of high school athletes. Through injury prevention strategies, prompt injury assessments, and appropriate rehabilitation protocols, you contribute to their physical health and help them recover from setbacks. Additionally, by providing a compassionate ear, offering words of encouragement, and fostering a safe and inclusive environment, you have the power to positively impact their emotional well-being and contribute to their overall growth and resilience.

Mentoring and Role Modeling:

As a student athletic trainer, you serve as a mentor and role model for high school athletes. Your dedication, work ethic, and passion for helping others inspire those around you. By embodying qualities such as integrity, empathy, and perseverance, you set an example that athletes can look up to. Through your actions and interactions, you have the power to influence their attitudes, behaviors, and aspirations. By fostering a culture of respect, teamwork, and sportsmanship, you contribute to the positive development of young athletes and help shape their character both on and off the field.

Building Relationships and Trust:

Building strong relationships based on trust and mutual respect is fundamental to making a positive impact. By cultivating meaningful connections with athletes, coaches, and healthcare professionals, you create an environment of support and collaboration. When athletes trust in your expertise, guidance, and genuine care, they are more likely to seek help, adhere to treatment plans, and embrace the necessary steps for recovery and growth. Through open communication, active listening, and genuine empathy, you foster an atmosphere where athletes feel valued, understood, and empowered.

Making a positive impact on the lives of others is at the heart of being a student athletic trainer. Serving as a mentor and role model and building relationships based on trust, you have the power to shape the lives of high school athletes in profound ways. Embrace the opportunity to make a difference and let the joy and fulfillment that come from positively impacting the lives of others fuel your passion for serving as a student athletic trainer.

CHAPTER 8

CHALLENGES FACED BY STUDENT ATHLETIC TRAINERS

Managing Time and Priorities

One of the biggest challenges faced by student athletic trainers is managing their time and priorities effectively. Student athletic trainers must balance their academic responsibilities with those of a trainer. They often have to work long hours and juggle multiple tasks at the same time. While maintaining their academic performance, student athletic trainers must ensure quality care to the student.

To manage their time and priorities effectively, student athletic trainers must be organized and efficient. Creating a schedule or to-do list to help them manage their tasks, as well as setting clear goals and deadlines for themselves can ease the workload and help them visualize all the tasks/assignments they must complete before the next game.

Working with a Variety of Individuals

Another challenge faced by student athletic trainers is working with a variety of individuals with varied expectations. Everyone has their own unique needs and perspectives, and it can be challenging for the trainers to communicate them. The trainers have to work very subtly while developing confidence in the student athletes. There can be challenges that will have to be overcome through communication, analytical thinking and with time management.

Balancing Academic and Extracurricular Responsibilities

Finally, student athletic trainers must balance their academic and extracurricular responsibilities effectively. While providing care and support for student-athletes is a crucial part of their role, they must also maintain their academic performance and fulfill their other responsibilities as students. They may need to sacrifice some of their extracurricular activities to focus on their academic performance or vice versa. Additionally, they must be able to communicate effectively with their coaches and other healthcare professionals, ensuring that their academic responsibilities are not compromised by their responsibilities as a student athletic trainer.

CHAPTER 9

WHAT IS IN MY BAG?

F inally, the most important part and parcel of a Student Athletic Trainer!

Student athletic Trainer is incomplete and ineffective unless he/ she is carrying a fully stocked medical aid bag with immediate supplies to treat an injury during practices and competitions. Caring for the athletes is the prime responsibility of the trainer and being able to provide first-aid is the foremost obligation. A well-prepared bag for a well-cared athlete is where the training starts from.

1. First Aid Supplies:

A well-stocked kit is the necessity of every student athletic trainer's game bag. Ensure that your kit includes adhesive bandages, sterile gauze pads, hydrogen peroxide wipes, adhesive tape (I like to carry one roll of athletic tape, a lot of self-adhesive tape, and one roll of stretch tape), scissors, and disposable gloves. It is important to regularly check and replenish your supplies to ensure that everything is up to date and readily available when needed. There have been many times where I have been on the field and not had enough tape to cover a turf burn. Athletic tape is very good for preliminary taping. You will find the power flex is excellent for on-field injuries. It takes less time to apply and is durable to last through a few plays.

2. Injury Prevention Tools:

This may include items such as athletic tape, pre-wrap, ankle braces, knee braces, and protective padding. These tools can be used to provide support, stability, and protection to athletes during practices and games. Normally, these will be in the kit that is brought out to the sideline. For our school, we have an extremely large kit with everything that we could need. With that being said, if you run out of tape and don't have time to go get it from the training room, use the tape that is brought down and in the big kit.

3. Water and Snacks:

Carry a water bottle or hydration pack to ensure you have access to fluids throughout practices and games. Additionally, consider packing healthy snacks like energy bars, fruits, or nuts to provide quick fuel for athletes during breaks. There have been many times where I have not brought a snack with me to eat on the bus and I had to get something from the concession stand. Game days can be very long. Typically at our school, our Gameday procedures start at 2 o'clock. Moving around from place to place and getting everything ready for the Friday night can be very laborious. You forget to eat and reminding yourself to eat and drink water is very important.

4. Communication Devices:

Effective communication is crucial for coordinating with coaches, healthcare professionals, and other members of the sports medicine team. Carry a fully charged cell phone in your game bag to stay connected and easily reach out for assistance if needed. Ensure that you have important contact numbers saved for quick access. Big injuries can happen and there can be times where you Athletic Director will not be there. It is important to make sure you inform them of any injury that happens when they are not there so they can take care of the precautions the next day.

5. Personal Protective Equipment (PPE):

It is important to prioritize safety and hygiene. Carry personal protective equipment, such as disposable gloves and hand sanitizers, to protect yourself and others from potential infections. Adhere to the guidelines and protocols set by your school or sports organization regarding the use of PPE. It is very important to wear gloves when handling blood. Everybody is watching it especially when an injury happens. Not only will you be liable for anything that happens but also the school. Sanitizing your hands after dealing with an injury or even rehab is crucial.

Being well-prepared and equipped with the necessary items is essential for student athletic trainers to provide effective care and support to high school athletes. Your game bag should include first aid supplies, injury prevention tools, hydration and nutrition items, communication devices, and personal protective equipment.

By ensuring that you have the essential items with you at the field, you can confidently handle various situations and contribute to the overall well-being and safety of the athletes you serve.

CHAPTER 10

EMERGENCIES

E mergencies can happen at any time during practices or games, and being prepared to take swift and appropriate action is paramount.

1. Emergency Preparedness:

Being prepared for emergencies is the foundation of effective response. Familiarize yourself with the emergency action plan established by your school or sports organization. Understand the roles and responsibilities of each member of the sports medicine team during emergencies. Ensure that emergency contact information, including the contact details of healthcare professionals and local emergency services, is readily available.

2. Assessing the Situation:

When an emergency arises, quickly assess the situation to determine the severity and nature of the injury or illness. Remain calm and approach the situation with a clear mind. Ensure the safety of the athlete and those around you and take necessary steps to prevent further harm. Evaluate the need for immediate medical attention and communicate the situation to appropriate personnel. Sometimes, you won't even be needed in the situation, but providing aid to other players that may be seeing what is happening is crucially as important. HIPAA guidelines forbid you from telling other players what may be going on, so the best answer that you could tell them is that you don't know what is happening.

3. Activating Emergency Services:

If the situation requires immediate medical assistance, activate the emergency medical services (EMS) by dialing the emergency phone number. Provide accurate and concise information about the location, nature of the emergency, and any specific instructions from the emergency action plan. Stay on the line until instructed to hang up and follow any guidance given by the EMS operator. This situation happens very rarely. In my 4 years of training, I have yet to dial 911. If it becomes a situation where you are the one to dial 911, remain calm on the line.

4. Providing Initial Care:

While waiting for medical professionals to arrive, provide appropriate initial care based on your training and scope of practice. This may include cardiopulmonary resuscitation (CPR), controlling bleeding, stabilizing fractures, or dislocations. Remain focused and follow the principles of first aid and emergency care. Remember that you will not be the only one helping the injured athlete. You will have your coaches, other members of sports, medicine, and possibly players help. Using what you have, and what you know, make sure you give this player the best treatment you possibly can.

Responding to emergencies requires quick thinking, decisive action, and a calm demeanor. As a student athletic trainer, you play a vital role in ensuring the well-being and safety of high school athletes during emergencies. By being prepared, assessing situations effectively, activating emergency services, providing initial care, communicating with stakeholders, and offering post-emergency follow-up, you contribute to a comprehensive and coordinated response. Your dedication and training in emergency response make a significant impact on the lives of athletes, instilling confidence in their safety and fostering a culture of care in the program.

CONCLUSION

Being a student athletic trainer has been one of the most profound and fulfilling experiences of my life. It is not just about treating injuries or preventing them, it is about the bonding I have with the athletes and coaches. Being a part of the sports program has allowed me to witness firsthand the dedication, hard work, and passion that goes into each game and practice. I have seen athletes push themselves to their limits, overcome obstacles, and achieve their goals. It has been an honor to be a part of their journey and to provide support and care along the way.

The relationships that I have developed with the athletes are one of the most rewarding aspects of being a student athletic trainer. I understand the importance of having a support system that believes in you and encourages you to do your best. As a student athletic trainer and friend, I have been able to provide that support and care to the athletes I work with. I have seen them grow and develop not only as athletes but also as individuals. It is incredible to see the impact that sports can have on their lives, and I am proud to be a part of that journey.

Working with coaches has been an invaluable experience for me. Coaches are an essential part of the sports program, providing guidance, motivation, and leadership to the athletes. I have had the opportunity to work closely with coaches, collaborating with them to develop training plans and injury prevention strategies. I have learned a lot from their experience and expertise, and I am grateful for their support and mentorship as I continue to carry on those skills with me through my walk of life.

In addition to the athletes and coaches, I have also had the privilege of working with other healthcare professionals, such as physical therapists, to coordinate care for injured athletes and ensure a safe and timely return to play. I have had the opportunity to educate student-athletes on proper nutrition, hydration, and injury prevention techniques. This has allowed me to develop my communication and teamwork skills, which are essential for any healthcare professional.

Being a student athletic trainer has allowed me to connect with the sports, athletes, and coaches in a meaningful way. It has been a privilege to be a part of the sports program and to contribute to the success of high school sports. I am grateful for the experiences I have had and the relationships I have developed, and I look forward to continuing to make a positive impact on the lives of others through sports. Being a student athletic trainer has not only allowed me to pursue my passion for helping others but has also given me the opportunity to learn and grow as an individual. It is a profession that has enriched my life in countless ways, and for that, I am truly grateful.

Watching the lights on the field turn off after the end of every season is always heart wrenching, win or loss. All the hard work both trainers and athletes have put as has paid off and a new chapter and journey begins. The rewarding and happy yet sad and disappointing feeling after the end of every season is something I cannot put into words. You must be there to experience it and when you do, it is worth every single second.

ACKNOWLEDGEMENTS

Writing a book is a journey that goes beyond the words on the page. It is with immense gratitude and heartfelt appreciation that I acknowledge the individuals whose unwavering support and encouragement made this endeavor possible.

First and foremost, I extend my deepest gratitude to my family. Their endless love, understanding, and belief in me have been the bedrock of my journey. They have cheered me on through the ups and downs, providing the strength and motivation to keep pushing forward.

I am indebted to my mentors, teachers, and professors, whose guidance and knowledge have shaped my understanding of sports medicine. Your passion for education and willingness to share your expertise have been invaluable in shaping this book.

To the athletes who have allowed me to be a part of their journey, thank you for the inspiration and trust you placed in me as a student athletic trainer. Your determination and dedication have been a constant reminder of the impact that sports medicine can have on individuals' lives.

I extend my gratitude to the sports medicine team and coaching staff for their collaboration and support. Your teamwork and camaraderie have made every practice and game an opportunity for growth and learning.

A special acknowledgment goes to my friends and fellow student athletic trainers. Your camaraderie and shared experiences have made this journey more memorable and enjoyable.

I am thankful to the readers of this book, whose interest in the world of sports medicine has motivated me to share my knowledge and experiences. I hope this book serves as a valuable resource for aspiring athletic trainers and enthusiasts alike.

Lastly, to everyone who has played a role, big or small, in the creation of this book, thank you. Your contributions have shaped its essence and enriched its content. I am truly humbled and honored to have had your support on this journey.

With gratitude,
Nanaki Matharu

Made in the USA
Middletown, DE
25 September 2023